Case 101

I0462582

Robert Larios

11/31/13

Period 5

Prologue

Once, there was a guy named Ward House. He was the top student at his school. Ward always wanted to work for the CIA. Currently, he lives in Cuba with his family: his mom, dad, sister, brother, and dog, Chewie.

Ward is strong. He can bench 90 pounds without breaking a sweat. Weight lifting helps him think, but sometimes he thinks too much and his body hurts afterwards. Everyone who knows him has seen him be kind, and most of his friends think he is cool.

He already has won the Nobel Prize two times! One for the Peace Award and the other one for math. He is 16 years old and likes to wear a tee-shirt with shorts. His room is covered with medals and trophies he has won. He has many books about law and justice and when he immerses himself in them, the room becomes so silent, that a bug can be heard. Unfortunately, Ward has an enemy named Karol.

Karol Jason is 17 years old, with blue eyes and brown hair. His room is a mess and is disorganized. It smells like a pig. He has posters that inspire him to be like the Naxis and Osama Bin Laden. One can hear the souls in that room. In the room one can taste the food that he has on the floor. He lives in New York, and also goes to school with Ward. Karol gets easily angry if one touches him. He would turn on fire if he could! Karol never had a big family because his parents got killed by an unknown man who shot them. After the incident, he becomes a hard, cold, blooded kid who does not like anyone. Karol can become so mad that if he could he would throw fire from his mouth.

Chapter 1

Junior Year

In the eleventh grade Karol had friends, family, and love from others. His life was going good, but Ward had come from Cuba and everyone thought that he was better than Karol. Every time that Karol had new things Ward would have better things. Whenever

Karol would be in class with Ward, Ward would take up all the attention from Karol. One day in class Karol got really mad and decides to confront him.

After the confrontation Ward throws Karol a baseball at his face and goes running to his mommy. Karol's house was in a neighborhood where there was a lot of stealing and drug dealing, it was a bad influence. When he got home, his mom and dad were drunk. They both started arguing about something and Karol never found out what they were fighting for. They went outside to deal with the problem and saw a man stealing stuff from a girl so Karol's parents went to help her. Karol's parents saw the person with a gun and they got shot along with the girl. Karol didn't realize about the incident until the next day, which was 11:00 p.m., already. He was in the house eating when he saw that his parents had not come back from the fight. He saw the clock and it was 12:00 p.m. Karol then called his Uncle, Jack to tell him about his parents and Jack tells him, "Do not go anywhere, I will be there as fast as I can." Jack got there and saw cops in Karol's house.

Jack tells the cops, "I am his Uncle Jack."

The police says, "Sir, I am really sorry, but the parents of Karol Jason have died by an unknown man who shot them. They also tell him everything that happened."

Uncle Jack takes Karol to his house to live with him and tells him about the incident. Karol cried and cried, and could not believe what he was going through. Over the year Jack fed him, bought him clothes, and became a parent to him. Karol continued to go to school, but it was never the same because he did not have the support of his parents. Karol becomes a bad kid in school. He gets pure F's in school and begins to say bad words when Ward is around. Karol thinks that his life has ended.

Jack tells him, "Karol do not worry, everything is fine."

Karol quietly says, "Jack it is over, everything is mess up for me. Why does it have to happen to me?"

Karol also says, "Jack, you know that I am useless to do anything because my grades stink, my life is ruined, and I don't even have parents, which everyone in school mostly has."

Jack was shocked because he thought that everything was fine with Karol. He kept on trying to help him, but one day Karol got a knife and almost killed himself. Jack was so scared, but had to overcome that and rushed Karol to stop him from committing suicide. Jack tells him about how his life is not over yet. Karol, after a while, goes back to school and starts to see Ward.

Ward goes up to Karol, with his eyes red, tells Ward, "Get away!"

Ward angrily says, "What! I did not do anything to you, Karol. I was just going to apologize to you about the day I threw you a baseball."

Karol says, "Well, I do not accept your apology because you are the one that made me lose my parents and everything!"

Karol runs to his class and Ward goes after him. Ward was telling him that he was very sorry for everything, but he did not know about Karol losing his parents. Karol did not want to listen to Ward's excuses and tells the teacher that if he can go to the restroom. Karol went to the restroom, but instead of going there, he goes home. Ward looks at the clock, 20 minutes had past, and he then tells the teacher if he can go look for Karol. The teacher, Mrs. Gook, told him that he can go and to come back quickly. Ward went to the restroom and found a letter. Ward reads the letter and this is what it said

Dear, Ward House

I know who sent the killer of Karol's parents. Ward, I know you so believe this letter because if you don't then Karol will never talk to you ever again. So back to Karol's parents, they were killed by a guy that was drunk and shot Karol's parents. The cops never caught the murderer and I know everything that you need to know. If you believe me then go to the park, near the trashcans at 7:30 p.m. don't be late!

Sincerely, Mystery Guy

Ward was stunned because he saw that Karol was not in the restroom and got shocked mostly from the letter. He goes back to the classroom and tells the teacher that Karol had to leave school due to a medical problem.

Mrs. Gook says, "Do you seriously think I am going to believe that?"

Ward responds, "Well call the office, they will say that he left home."

Mrs. Gook calls the office and the office tells her that he left home running. Mrs. Gook thought that someone had picked him up, but she was wrong, he ditched school.

Ward starts investigating the case throughout the day and finds some stuff like about the problems that Karol had with his parents and also how they treated him. Ward then saw a file on the principal's desk that was a paper of Karol's parents that said, **"Karol Jason adopted in the New Hampshire."** Ward was shocked because he saw the things that Karol went through. There were pictures of his childhood and throughout his teenage years. He also saw a note that said, "Real parents of Karol found died in Vermont." Ward was about to see more stuff, but then he hears sound coming in the room so he hides under the desk. Then the principal, Mr. Dool, goes inside for his cup of coffee that he had left behind and then leaves after that. Ward then took the files and left the room before anyone else found out.

Ward was walking to math class when he sees Karol, but when he went to check out if it was Karol, he was not there anymore.

Ward was confused and asked an eighth grade kid, "Did you see a kid that passed by through here just now ago." The kid says, "No, there was no kid here, it was only me and my food. Why you ask?"

Ward then says, "I am sorry, continue to eat your food, Thank you, anyway." Ward goes to math class and after that he goes home.

Chapter 2

Meanwhile, when Ward was there, Karol was at home thinking about planning to kill Ward, for what he did. He played a video game about killing zombies on his Xbox. Karol was pumped up to kill people. He also went to eat chips to concentrate on the plan that he was making. He took about 2 hours to plan it all out. Karol was mad because he could not do the killing at the moment so he left the house and went to hide the knife for tomorrow. Karol throws the knife in one of the bushes that was near the school and left quickly to his house.

Ward, without knowing, passes through there and sees Karol, but does not say anything because he was going to the park for more evidence about Karol and his parents. When Ward went to the spot where he had been told to be, he saw Karol from distance, hiding something in the bush. When Karol left, Ward went to check out what it was. He finds the knife that Karol was hiding. Ward picked up the knife. He becomes scared because it had a carving of his name and said to himself, "I bet he tried to kill, but needed a plan so he can kill me."

Ward then saw a guy that was standing in the location where he was suppose to meet the mystery guy so he began to go over there.

Wards goes over, when he got there the guy tells him, "Are you the guy named Ward."

Ward says, "Yes, what is your name, guy?"

The guy says, "Well, my name is Bob Polk."

Ward then started telling him about who killed Karol's parents, which were the adopted parents. Bob says that he will tell him in time, but first he has to tell him about Ward's personal stuff.

Ward says, "Why do you need to know about me?"

Bob says, "Because I need to know if you are not a fake."

Ward tells him, "You know that no one else would know this, except us two."

Bob then says, "Ok, OK I will tell you who killed them."

Ward interrupts Bob before he tells him who killed Karol's parents and says, "What if you are telling a lie?"

Bob responds, "Well if you do not believe me, then you will never find out who killed them."

Bob adds, "It was your uncle!"

Ward was stunned and speechless. Then after two minutes of silence, Ward says, "I do not believe you, I know my uncle and he would not kill a fly."

Bob says, "It was him because I saw him clearly with my two big eyes."

Bob also says, "I hope this will help you, but if it does not help you then go somewhere else to look for other answers. See you around." He then disappeared in the bushes.

Ward was left puzzled with the case of Karol's parents and started to go home, to work on the plan to kill Ward, but was getting late so he had to do that at his house.

When he got home he started going through the files to see if it was really his uncle. Ward was looking at the files when his mom called him to go eat.

Ward says, "Mom, I am not hungry right now, I am doing my homework, but thanks."

Ward's dad, Dave, checks on Ward when he was going to the bathroom. Ward then tells his dad, "Is my Uncle Fort doing well today?"

His dad says, "Yes, he is alright."

Ward started to tell him a lot of question about his uncle.

His dad, Dave tells him, "Why are you so interested in your Uncle Fort?"

Ward tells Dave, "Well, because I want to know more about my Uncle Fort so I can spend more time with him."

Dave tells his son, "Son, do you really want to know about your Uncle Fort?"

Ward says, "Yes."

Dave responds, "Well, let's see he was a drinker, used firearms, and also had a habit to go to the casino to waste his few dollars."

Ward was just listening and couldn't believe what he had just heard.

Dave continues, "He would go to the discos and enjoyed overdosing on his pills. Is that enough information about your Uncle Fort or would you want more?"

Ward says, "Yes, that is enough, thank you Dad."

Dave then got up and left. Ward then started to write this all down and tried to remember all the things that Bob told him. Then all the sudden the phone rings and Ward's mom answers it. His mom tells Ward that it was his uncle and that his dad had to go to his house now. Dave left quickly to see what was wrong with his brother, but before he left, Ward tagged along with him.

When they got to his Uncle's house they found a lot of broken stuff. They quickly ran inside and found his brother down on the ground. He appeared to been stabbed and was bleeding too much that they had to take him to the hospital.

Ward stayed at his Uncle's house to search the house. He finds a gun in his Uncle Fort's room and also a knife in the trashcan with fresh blood on it. Ward sees the memories of his Aunt Mary in a picture, which died a few years back. He then goes to find other stuff.

Chapter 3

Back at the hospital, Dave was so worried about Fort, his brother, and thinking about who would do such a thing.

Dave tells the nurse "Is my brother going to be ok."

The nurse says, "Well, the injury is really bad, but he can survive. We will try our best, Sir."

Dave was ready to cry, but held it in because he didn't want to cry in front of the nurse. Dave was praying for his brother to get better and at least to able to speak, but nothing happened. Dave was so scared that he couldn't take it and went to get some coffee. The nurse asked the doctor that if the patient was going to make it. The doctor told her that it was too late. The nurse just stood there and saw the brother approached her. The nurse didn't know what to say and told him that he would be ok. Dave finally took a deep breath and could relax. He was getting really sleepy so he went to bed on the chair.

After a few hours of sleep, Dave knows that his brother is going to be alright so he tells the nurse, "I will be back in a few days to check up on him." He leaves to work from there.

Meanwhile, at the house of his brother, Ward discovered something else; he finds dirty, bloody clothes in the sink. Ward just examined the clothes and in those clothes he could see something shaped like a gun. He took a pair of gloves and took out the gun.

Ward was so scared that he almost dropped it. Ward opened a bag and put all of the evidence into the bag.

Later that day, Karol had a plan to kill Ward and get revenge for what he did. Karol starts to make a decoy to fool Ward. So he builds a robotic thing which looked like him.

Then his Uncle Jack calls him and tells him, "What happened in school today?

Karol tells him that, "It went good and I made some friends."

Jack tells him that, "I will be at home at 10:00 p.m. and tells Karol you should be in bed by then."

Karol adds, "Jack I promise, I will be in bed by then and see you tomorrow uncle."

Jack responds, "Alright I'll see you later."

Karol then starts to hurry up and finishes the robot. He then had to find a way to hide the robot from his uncle. Karol thought and thought, looked and looked, until he found a basement in the house that he knew about. He went in which was very dim and couldn't see anything until he saw a light bulb hanging on the ceiling and turned it on. Karol looked around and found a book of memories that said, "To you Jack and forever and ever." Karol looked at it and opened it.

He found a lot of stuff from his parents, but it was mostly about his Aunt Star. There was a lot of mini paragraph on the picture on the back. There was one that said, "Jack I know that you love me, but I need some time to think of what you have done to me, Love Star." Then another that said, "Star why did you leave me, I have been so bad to you that I will make it up to you, I am really, really, really, really sorry, hope you understand, Love Jack." Karol got surprised because he didn't know that his aunt left Jack. He looked at the clock and it was 9:50 p.m. He then hurried up to find a place to store the robot and found a closet that had a broom in there so he stored it in there. Karol heard a sound coming to the door and turned off the lights; he closed the door, and started to run towards the room. It was his Uncle Jack. He went to bed right after Jack went to check on him. After that Jack went downstairs to take a shower and went to bed.

Chapter 4

The next day, Jack went to work at 3:00 a.m. and Karol got up at 5:30 a.m. to go see the robot. It was there and could tell that Jack did not come down to the basement. He then took it upstairs to make it more like him by putting clothes on it and covering the face. He finally was going to finish, but the phone was ringing and he answered. It was Ward and he asked him that how he had the phone number of Karol.

Ward says, "Karol listen to me I didn't do what you think I did."

Karol tells him, "I don't believe anything you say, do not call me anymore!"

Ward replies, "Karol look I am really sorry that you think that, but I have to tell you that you're..." Karol had smashed the phone into the ground and went to kill Ward.

When Karol was going to school, one of the kids looked at his robot and says, "That's pretty cool."

Karol impatiently says, "Get away! I will kill you if you say another word." The kid started running like a little boy. Karol hurried to school and put the robot in a janitor's closet. He went for the knife, which was in the bush, but when he went for it was not there. He started looking everywhere for it and finally he says to himself in a low voice, "Could I of misplaced it?"

Karol was getting mad and saw Ward walking to class; he knew it was his only chance to assassinate him. So he hid in the bushes and waited for Ward to arrive. He then ran to his locker and took out a special kind of soap. Karol intended to get Ward's eyes for Ward to not see for a while and to have time to find the missing knife. Ward was going to the lab and Karol ran towards him. Ward saw Karol with the corner of his eye and jumped and kicked Karol on to the ground. The soap went up into the air and, without knowing, Ward caught the soap. He asked Karol where he was at and why was he running with soap. Karol just stood up and ran to the janitor's closet. He used a paperclip to lock the closet door. Ward just stood there wondering.

Ward told the office that there was a boy in there and he had locked the door. The principal goes to get the master key to open the closet. When they got there and opened it, there was nothing there not even a boy. Ward explained to Mr. Nort that it was true there was someone there.

Mr. Nort tells him, "Ward you are going to get in big trouble if you are lying."

Ward rapidly says, "Mr.Nort go look at the cameras you will see a guy leaving the closet at 1:45 or around then."

Mr. Nort says, "OK fine I will go look at the video monitors just because you have A's."

He goes to his office with Ward and they see someone running out of the closet, but Ward could not tell if it was Karol.

Mr. Nort asks Ward, "What is the name of the boy."

Ward tells him in a low voice that it is Karol Jason. Mr. Nort gets surprised because when he left from the school for a year that boy was an anti bad boy and he was a straight A's kid. Ward tells Mr. Nort that when Karol's parents die it went downhill from there. Ward also tells him that Karol is now living with his uncle and he thinks that all this was because of me.

Mr. Nort tells Ward, "Do not worry, we will fix all this." Then the secretary calls up Mr. Nort to go to a meeting and tells Ward to come tomorrow.

Ward goes to class and thinks about the poor kid. He gets distracted from it so much that he gets a B+ on his AP Science exam. When he got out of the school he went home and started going to Jack's house. When he crossed through the graveyard and passed the bridge he saw Karol going into this old abandoned house. He went to the old house and through the window, that was very dirty, saw Karol working on this robot that looked like Karol. Karol was working on the robot to make him speak. He almost got it to work, but he put in the wrong microchip because it malfunctioned. Ward was seen everything and when Karol went to get the right chip he went in. Ward saw the plans to kill someone which he thought it was him of course and looked at the robot. He put a tracking chip on it and left quickly. Ward took a picture of the plans. He also wrote on the plans to kill him and put the wrong information. Then Ward left to his house.

Ward got home and his parents told him with an angry voice, "Where were you at Ward?"

Ward says, "Um mm, at a friend's house helping him get a better grade in AP Science."

His mom tells him, "See how honest you can be, it was a question that was not that difficult to answer."

Ward tells her, "I will be going to my room because I am having tons of homework to do, bye." Ward ran up stairs and went to his room to work on the case a bit more. He had found a clue about

Karol's life. When he was a baby he got abused by his biological parents who were from Cuba. He knew about the cruelty he was towards Cubans. Ward looked at the picture he took and downloaded onto the computer. He could see that his plans were to capture him when he goes to school early. Ward saw the location of Karol's opening plan which was going to school first, then hiding in the bushes and putting the robot to talk with Ward; next Karol will come from behind and kill Ward. Ward, to himself, says, "That will never happen because I am one step ahead of him."

Karol got to assemble the robot with the chip and he starts to record his voice so it would sound like him. He also put another feature which was a secret knife/gun on the boot and also on the wrist. He tests all of the stuff on his dummy and delivered promising results, but when Jack got home he heard a lot of noise so he ran towards Karol's room.

Jack knocks on the door and Karol quietly tells him, "I am sorry; I was only testing out a project for science."

Jack tells him, "OK, just keep it down over there."

Jack then goes to go eat something and watches some T.V. while he was eating. Karol was almost done with everything except he had to do one last thing which was to make everything seem real. So he had to use his coat to cover the gun under his hand and had to cover the knife with a pair pants. He was very sleepy, but could not go to sleep until he had the basic parts for the killing.

Then Jack went to take a shower and knocks on Karol's door.

He tells him, "Karol you should get some shut eye for tomorrow." Karol just turned off the lights, but used his lamp to see. He ended up finishing the project at 1:00 a.m.

The next breezy day, Dave went to go see his brother in the hospital. Ward got up like at 7:30 a.m. and had to make some makeshifts to his original plan. Ward then left for school. Dave could not go to work because he had come late from the hospital.

Earlier that day, Ward was waiting for him to pop up out of nowhere, but nothing happened so he wondered if Karol had found out if he had been looking at him the whole time when he was investigating. He looked everywhere for him, but until 10 minutes later, he had found him at the end of the bus stop. Karol was just standing there with an old tee-shirt and baggy pants. Ward went to hide for Karol not to see him and Karol started to come towards his way. Ward knew that his only chance to talk to him was now or never. So when Karol stepped onto the curb, Ward jumped towards him and tackled him to talk to him. Ward took him to the office and told Mr. Nort to talk to him about his assassination towards Ward.

Mr. Nort tells Ward, "Why did you do this to his boy?"

Ward utters, "Well to get the truth out of him."

Mr. Nort got angry and tells Ward, "Ward I know that you never get detention, but you will need to have one."

Ward stood there and felt sorry for doing his. Ward whispered to Karol about how he was sorry for wrapping him and accepted the consequence. Mr. Nort wrote the detention and took Ward to the main office. Then Mr. Nort discussed about the killing of Ward and Karol denied everything.

He tells Mr. Nort, "Mr. Nort why are you accusing me of killing someone if he have not seen me kill a fly, but I do have a lot of ditching in my reckoned in this school."

Mr. Nort responds, "I am sorry if I offended you, I should be ashamed because I believed a guy that had straight A's, just because you are smart does not mean you have the power to be telling people what they should do. I am truly sorry; you may now go to your class. Have a good day."

Karol then left with a grin on his face and had Mr. Nort on his side. Karol went to math class and on his way he put a device on Ward's backpack. That device was to detect where Ward is at, at all times.

Karol then sat in a chair and the math teacher, Mrs. House, tells him, "How good of you to make it today, with a smile."

Karol just stared at her and Mrs. House told everyone to take out their math books. Karol took out his and these boys started to tell him mean stuff. Karol got really mad after a while and told them off. Mrs. House got up and told him to go to the main office. Karol refused to go and he sat in his desk. Mrs. House was forced to call the office and send the principal to come and get him.

Mr. Nort was surprised to see the student that he agreed with last time they met. Mr. Nort talked with Karol about what happened and then he brought Karol lunch to tell him more. Karol tells Mr. Nort that he is the kindness teacher or principal than any other person he has met. Mr. Nort started talking to him about how he had problems with school, but overcame those things. He overcame those bad things by just ignoring them. Mr. Nort also tells him about why you should think positive and not negative stuff. Karol starts telling him about the situation he was in at home and in school.

Mr. Nort tells him, "Karol whenever you need help just come by my office."

Karol then agreed to the idea and left to his house because it was already 4:30 p.m. When he got home he went straight to the old abandoned house to work on the GPS tracker on Ward.

Ward was at home studying when he overheard his dad crying on the couch. He asked his dad what was wrong and his dad says, "Well your Uncle Fort has died just recently and we will need money for his funeral."

Ward started to cry also because he knew that without him there would be no evidence for who really killed Karol's parents. Dave then left outside to go somewhere.

After a while, Karol got it to work and he was able to track Ward's location. Karol then set his timer to go off at 6:30 a.m. and left the house. When he got to his uncle's house he didn't find Jack anywhere. He checked everywhere, but he had not looked in the basement. So he went there and he found him there. He quietly entered and Jack was writing another letter to his aunt, from the looks of it. Karol then left upstairs to go eat something. Karol wanted a sandwich so he started by getting the soft bread, then getting the dried mayo and the wilted lettuce, next he went to get the wet ham, after that he got the sour tomato, finally he toasted the sandwich and he had just made himself dinner. Karol then got a diet soda and began to eat. Jack found Karol eating and just went to sleep. Karol after finishing washed his plate and went to take shower. Then he went to bed for the big day waiting him tomorrow.

In that night Karol could not sleep from the next day that had been stored for him on the next day. Karol started doing and list of things of what might he do to Ward. He also did a planned if the police started to find where he is. He knew after the killing he must hide somewhere safe, so he started to think of places that were a possibility. Karol also thought about not doing it. His conscious started to tell him not to do this because he was going to ruin his life, but the evil began to creep on him and there was no way out of this. Karol thought about Jack and if he was the guy that left Aunt Star or the secret guy that nobody wanted to be noticed, but Karol had found out about the problem. He fell asleep when he was saying that and didn't want to wake up at 6:30 a.m., but had to anyway.

Chapter 5

The next day, Karol had been eating cereal when suddenly he remembered about the tracking device. He ran to the old house and found the tracking device beeping, which meant that Ward was on the move. Ward was going to school. Karol then gets the robot and goes off to school. Karol arrives to school and immediately goes to the gym, towards his locker and gets the rat poison. Karol's plan was set, he was to poison Ward then kill him by making Ward suffer for what he had done. Ward was walking by the gym when the robot was going towards him and Ward immediately is fooled and thinks that the robot is Karol, so he started talking to him.

Ward surprised tells the robot Karol, "Karol how have you been and I am very sorry for wrapping you up like that, do you accept my apologize?"

Robot Karol with a rough voice says, "I do not accept it, leave now or suffer."

Ward got puzzled from what he said and tells him, "What do you mean Karol?"

Robot Karol tells him with an angry voice, "Leave or suffer!!!"

Ward gets the idea of what robot Karol was saying because he had remembered the plan, that he found in the house and started to go along with it until robot Karol would go away. Robot Karol gets near him and uses the boot knife to stab him. Robot Karol gets to him and Ward has a pan, that he brought from his house, to block the knife. Robot Karol strikes him, but Ward's reflexes reacted in time and blocked it. Ward then ran to safety towards the office. The real, which was not the robot, Karol jumped from the bushes and started chasing Ward. Karol gets his leg with a hand knife and Ward struggles to run, but manages to reach the office. Ward tells the office about the incident then they called the police, but it was too late because Karol was nowhere to be found.

The police ask Ward, "What happened? How does the look like?"

He tells them, "There was a kid that stabbed me and ran away before you guys arrived."

The police went to Karol's house and Ward was sent to the hospital because of the uncontrollable bleeding. The office then contacted Ward's parents.

When Ward got to the hospital they tried to stop the bleeding, but it was much worse than what they thought, because when they took off the knife it left pieces of metal and wire. The doctors had to make a decision of either to perform surgery or of cutting off his leg if the bleeding would not stop. Ward was scared because he saw a lot of blood, the doctors then decided to put on a gas mask. His parents had arrived and got notified about the problem. They were very worried because their son was in the emergency room.

Meanwhile, the police had arrived in Karol's house because would go to the old house. The police did not know until the office had called them. Then they went in Jack's house, but no one was there, not even Karol. So they blew up the door and cautiously went in one by one. They had found guns and knives in the basement. The police went upstairs and found wires and metals in a room. They also found gunshots in another room and blood in the bathroom.

They searched every single inch to find Karol, but they were unsuccessful. They waited until the owner arrived back from work. They waited and waited, and finally they saw a car coming from a distance. It was Jack, but before he opened the door the police stopped him.

They ask Jack, "Who are you? Where are you coming from? Where is your nephew, Karol Jason?

Jack explains everything and tells them, "Police, I do not know where is Karol because he always gets here very late."

The police tell Jack about the problem that happened in school. They also tell Jack about Karol and the kid that he had hurt which was Ward. Jack could not believe it, but he had something to tell them which were the time that Karol tried to commit suicide after his parents had died.

Jack states, "Karol would be in this house, but I never knew where he was at."

Jack also says, "Karol would tell me that he was in his room. Karol also became interested in guns, all of the sudden."

The police wrote all this down and searched the house for one last time for anything that would help them.

After a few hours of searching they did not find anything and they decide to leave. They gave Jack a paper, which he read. It had all the things that people cannot do and can do. It also had a date where Jack has to go to trial and the trial will decide if Karol needs to go to jail.

That night at 11:30 p.m. Karol was coming from the secret hiding spot that he had. Karol went to Jack's house with caution as he stepped in. Karol did not see anyone or a cop so he went through the basement door. There he went to get food and clothes. He also got money from the safe that Karol already knew the combination to. Jack heard noise coming from the downstairs, so he got up and checks what was happening. Jack was going downstairs when Karol saw Jack from the corner of his left eye and disappeared in a blink of an eye. Jack was somewhat sleepy and he could not tell if it was Karol or not. Karol got all his stuff and went down to the basement. He ran out of the house super fast and went back to his secret place. Jack just closed the basement door and activates the alarm that he had installed. Karol did not know about this alarm.

Chapter 6

The morning of the next day, Ward had the operation to heal up all the injuries that they did to Ward. Ward could not sleep so the doctors gave him medicine to make him sleep in order to rest. His family was right there anytime he needed someone. Ward slept almost 11 hours! He woke up sore, which was usual, and was happy to see his family right there. Ward received food and the nurses would check up on him every hour or so. He would see the television, relax from school, and was sad at the same time because he knew who killed Karol's parents, but Karol was too mad at him to let him talk to him.

At that moment, Karol was at his secret place, which was an underground tunnel that he had found when his parents were around. He was thinking about what he going to do if the cops were trying to find him. Karol also thought if Ward was alive still he would get interrogate by the cops and Ward would tell them everything. They would tell him things like what had happened, what did Karol did to kill Ward, and a lot of other questions. Karol was eating the bread and butter that he stole from his uncle's house. He had stolen 1,800 dollars when he started counting it.

Then at Jack's house, Jack had to wake up at 8:30 a.m. and he called work so that Jack could explain to his boss what was happening to him.

His boss tells him, "Jack, why did you fail to come."

Jack responds, "Well I have some trouble with my nephew, so that is why I need an extra day off please."

His boss says, "Ok, but report to work at 3:00 A.M. tomorrow."

Jack replies, "Thank you, I will be there."

Jack then went to eat an egg muffin with coffee. Jack also took a shower and then he thought about yesterday. He tried to remember who the kid was. Jack thought, and thought until he came to a conclusion that it was Karol all along. Jack searched the room for any clues, but did not find anything. Jack also looked in this closet and saw that it was a robot that looked like Karol. Jack thought that Karol was hiding there, but when he touched him it was a robot.

The robot that Jack had found had something strange and says to himself, "Why did Karol do this, was the project he was working on or was this robot involved in the problem that happened yesterday?"

He takes out the robot from the closet and moves it to his room and starts to look for other items in the closet, but he only finds some other stuff like guns and knives attached to it.

Jack went to Karol's school and went to the main office. He wanted to speak with the principal, Mr. Nort. Mr. Nort tells Jack about what happened one day that Karol went to him and believed Karol.

Mr. Nort says, "It was about a problem with the same kid named, Ward which was the top student in the school, he had Karol wrapped up and I tell Ward that he would get a detention for doing that. Then I started talking with Karol because Ward tells him that he wanted to kill Ward. So I talked with Karol and he understood everything and he left fine, but I guess it was not like that."

Jack interrupts Mr. Nort and said, "Mr. Nort why didn't you believe Ward?"

Mr. Nort says, "Well because I thought that he was lying."

Jack says, "But you said he was the top student in the school."

Mr. Nort responds, "I thought that Karol was telling the truth this time."

Jack was very angry because what teacher or principal would believe a bad kid instead of a good, smart kid.

Jack tells Mr. Nort, "Mr. Nort, you are the dumbest principal in the entire world."

Jack then left and shuts the door with force. He went through the office and told off the ladies in the front desk in a low voice.

When he got to his car he went to the hospital with the kid named Ward. Jack was driving when he saw the cops going super fast to a house. He thought it could be Karol that they had found, so he went to look who it was.

When he arrived to the house and there were tons of cops around the house. He hid in a bush to hide from the cops so he would not get in trouble. The cops went in the house and when they were looking for someone like a guy, which fountarely was not Karol, ran to a police's car. The guy left with the tires screening on the ground. He went so fast that the cops did not realize. Jack knew what to do, which was going after the bad guy. He went to his car and started it. Jack then left to chase the bad guy. When he saw the car he started going faster and the guy didn't know that Jack was chasing him. Jack went faster than the guy and crashed into the car. The bad guy ran out of the police car and Jack chased him. Jack used the knife that he got from his car. The bad guy fell to the ground with a wounded leg.

The bad guy says, "What is wrong with you, bro."

Jack says, "Kid, you do stuff wrong then you do the time."

Then the police guys saw a cop car that was crashed and reported for more back up. When they got there Jack tells the police about what happened and how the car got crashed. The police then take the bad guy to a police car with blood running down his shirt and Jack was rewarded with a police car that the police gave him because his car was the one that saved the wanted guy. Jack got cleaned up and the medical people gave Jack a new shirt because it had too much blood on it. Jack was happy because he had a cool car. He decides to visit the hospital were Ward was staying at.

Chapter 7

Jack got there very late at night and, he asked the front desk where was Ward's room. The lady there tells Jack, "Sir, are you a family member to Ward?"

Jack says, "Yes I am his uncle."

The lady says, "Ok then, he is staying in room 232."

Jack says, "Thank you."

Jack rushed to Ward' room and went through the elevator to get there fast. When he got to 4th level he started looking for the numbers 200 through 250. He was looking through the rooms when a nurse was getting out of the room.

He asked the nurse, "Where's room 232."

The nurse says, "Take a left and it will be right there."

Jack speed walks towards the room. Jack went in the room.

When he went in the room he found Ward lying on the bed. Ward's parents were in the room sleeping. Jack did not want to wake up his parents. So he went to talk with Ward. Ward was waking up and Jack surprised him with a hug. Ward was freaking out because he did not know who was Jack at first.

Jack tells Karol, "I am Karol's uncle, Jack."

Ward was glad to see Karol's uncle because he could tell him about the situation between Karol and him. He did not want to tell him just yet.

Ward asks Jack, "How did it all being?"

Jack tells him, "Well, first they were fighting inside the house then they went outside to deal with the problem and a guy that was drunk killed them both. Also killed a woman that the parents of Karol were helping."

Ward starts talking about the murderer of Karol's parents, and wanted to know more about it.

Jack tells him, "I do not really know and nobody knows exactly either."

Jack talks to Ward about Karol trying to kill Ward.

Ward starts to tell him, "Karol thought that all this bad stuff that he was experiencing was my entire fault. I am from Cuba, but I came to the school to learn new stuff. Karol thought that I had taken his place as number one in the school. It was kind of my fault because I made him not like me. When I threw him a ball to his head area he ran to his mom. I felt really bad for doing the incident so I apologize the next day, but he was not the same. He acted like a different kid. Karol looked very down and would not get the same grades, which were A's. Overall had changed to a different kid from day to night."

Jack was very stunned because he was the top student in the school, but the killing affected him a lot.

Ward tells Jack, "Where is Karol now?"

Jack says, "Well the cops are after him now because of what happened at the school."

Ward tells him, "Jack, I think I know why my uncle killed Karol's parents."

Ward also adds, "It all makes sense now."

Jack with a curious voice says, "What do you mean, boy?"

Ward says in a rapid voice, "Well, the guy that gave me the information about my uncle was Bob and he knew a lot about him."

Ward tells Jack, "Bob told me in the park that my uncle had been a drinker, smoker, and someone who abused children, but what did not make sense was when he tells me, he also lived in two houses."

He also tells Jack, "I could not make up something about why he had two houses, but I knew why he said that because when he was around his family he would not do anything bad, but when my uncle would go to the other house, he would do bad stuff. It was just like giving me a hint that it really was my uncle."

Jack was kind of confused because from all that talking, it was too much to comprehend. Ward told him the whole thing, but slowly this time. Jack understood the things that Ward was trying to tell him and then the nurse came in. Jack had to leave because Ward's parents were waking up. Ward thanked Jack for coming. Jack then left before the nurse could realize.

The nurse tells Ward's parents, "Mr. and Mrs. House your son is ready to go home now, but you guys need to fill out some forms before you leave."

Ward's parents say, "Thank you, we will go get something to eat."

Then the nurse left and the parent's of Ward say to him, "Ward, would you like something before we leave to the buffet?"

Ward says, "Yes, I would like a sausage muffin with potato tots please and an orange juice."

Then they left with some money in her pocket. Ward got up and got a paper that Jack forgot to take. He started to open the letter when Jack came back with him. Ward got red faced and put the letter on his bottom. Jack says, "Ward did you see an envelope on that table over there."

Ward says, "Nope." Jack then left and went to find the paper.

Ward took out the letter and found money in it. He also found a chain in it too. Ward read the letter and it was to Jack's wife.

It says, "Dear Star, I love you, but I need you to come back for us two could find Karol or help me find him. He has been missing for 3 days now and he has not eaten anything, I think. Please come back I need you. I hope with this money will convince you to come back. I always love you. Love, Jack."

Ward was now even more scared because it was a letter to his wife saying to help him find Karol. He then put it into another envelope and put the same letter, but with a different handwriting. Ward then put the other envelope it in the middle of the magazines. He goes to find Jack to tell him that he had found it on the ground. Ward finally finds him. Jack was eating Chinese food.

Ward ran to him and tells him, "Jack I found it on the ground."

Jack says, "Thank you, I thought I lost this valuable thing."

Ward was curious and says, "What is in there?"

Jack utters, "Well stuff for someone, thank you, see you later."

He then left without eating everything on his plate. He appeared to be mad because when I handed him the letter he sounded angry. Ward then goes back to his room before his parents realize that he was gone.

When Ward got back, minutes later his parents got there with his breakfast. It had a plate of pancakes, a cup of oatmeal, hash browns, and a glass of orange juice. He then saw the food and started to eat like crazy. His parents were seeing him and were telling him to eat slowly because he could choke. Ward was done in 10 minutes.

Then his parents tells Ward, "Honey, were going to fill out the paper to go home."

Ward says, "Mom I want to go to the store in floor 1. So can I borrow some money from you?"

Ward's mom says, "Ok, but only 10 dollars."

Ward's parents then left to fill out those papers. Ward left to the store to buy something he wanted.

When he was going down to the first floor, he saw Karol going to another store outside of the hospital. Karol was running to this store, but it appeared to be abandoned. Ward wrote down on his arm the street address and then went to the store.

In the store, there was tons of junk food, drinks, candy, ice cream, and toys. He went to the junk section and chooses some Takis. He also got a Gatorade that was a 24 oz. It cost 4 dollars and he also got some Snickers. He was going back to the room with his favorite stuff. He was very happy to find a cool blue, Gatorade because lots of stores did not sell that drink anymore.

Ward got to the room and saw his parents were coming back when his mom says, "Let's go Ward we are leaving."

Ward was happy to leave so he can see some T.V. and go to school again.

They were leaving when their tire was flat. Ward went to the car and saw that the window was broken. His dad went to the front desk of the hospital and reported the case. The front office lady called the police right away and they came in 10 minutes. When the police were on their way, Ward was checking what the bad guys did to the car. He checked everything, but everything was in place. It did not appear that they want taken anything, but when Ward opened the back trunk and they had stolen his dad's I.D. card. So his dad could not enter his work without the I.D. card.

The police got there and they told them everything that they had stolen from them.

The police say, "Guys, we can only give you a car, but not the other stuff."

His dad says, "That is fine because I can get the other stuff from my work."

Then Ward and his family went with the police to get a new car. They got a semi new car and worked better than the other. They were happy and took all the other stuff from the old car to the new car. The police went inside of the hospital to check the video to see how did the bad guys break in the car or who. They saw the video and it was a man that took a hammer to break the window. This happened during the night time, it only took 2 minutes.

They then tell the family of Ward, "Guys we will be taking the car to the junkyard to tear it down." They did more stuff inside and then left to the junkyard.

Ward's family left the hospital with a cool car to his house. It was about one hour from there to get to his house, if there is no traffic. On their way they saw a car accident on the freeway. It was very nasty because it was four cars that crashed against each other and there were cops, ambulances, and firefighters on the scene. Ward was scared to imagine about himself being in that situation.

They were almost there and Ward turned up the music. He was signing when he saw a car going super fast and he was in the same lane that they were when...

In the Past

He started to remember the time when he was a little kid, when he would pull pranks on his parents and would not get in trouble.

He also remembered the time that his grandma died and tells him at the last moment, "Ward, I need to tell you something. You need to always remember this and never forgot his. Can you handle his task?"

Ward says, "Yes, I promise grandma."

His grandma says, "Well, I need to tell you that you must always love your family and especially your parents no matter what happens. You also must love the people that are always around you when they need help."

Ward was crying when he says, "Grandma, do not die, I always will love you and will love my parents, please grandma do not die."

His grandma says, "Ward I need to also tell you that you..."

She had died in that second that she was about to tell him something. Ward was very sad and wanted his grandma to come back because had only known her for about 2 years, from the ages 3 to 5 years old.

In the Present

Ward was out with a concussion and didn't know what was happening until his parents also woke up because they had hit the ground hard. They called the police and the ambulance. They waited about 2 minutes to take his son to the hospital and his mom goes with him. His dad waited for the police to investigate the crash.

On the ambulance the paramedics tried not to lose Ward and put oxygen into his mouth. His mom was very worried because first Ward had a leg injury and now this one. She looked at her son and prayed to God for her not to lose him. He was moving for the first time and it was a bit of a relief. They almost arrived to the hospital when Ward started to wake up and actually stood up a bit. As soon as the ambulance got there, they took him to a room and started to check everything. He was very exhausted from everything and fell asleep. They tried everything and they only found that he had a minor concussion.

They tell his mom, "Don't worry too much because he will be up in a few of hours when he is fully rested."

His says, "What about my husband that is out over there on the freeway."

They tell her, "Well, he will come over here after everything is sorted out."

She then went to Ward's room and waited until he woke up. He finally woke up in the morning and his parents were there to see him when he opened his eyes. He was happy to see his mom and dad there with him.

He tells his dad, "What happened to the cool car that they gave us?"

His dad says, "It got really crashed and it almost killed us, don't you remember?"

Ward says, "Nope."

His dad then thought that if Ward had a short term memory lost, it would be even worse. Ward's mom also went him her husband and told Ward to stay there. They were going to tell the doctor something, but the nurse told them that the doctor was not available.

They ask the nurse, "Well then does my son, Ward House, have a short term memory lost?"

The nurse says, "It appears that he does, why?"

His dad says, "Oh, because he could not remember the crash."

The nurse says, "Well when these crashes hit the head most of the people have concussions."

His dad says, "Thank you for telling us."

They then go to Ward's room. When they got there his son was telling them that he wanted to go home.

They tell him, "Ward we will go home as soon the doctor clears you, we can then go home."

Ward got a little mad because it was the second time he was there. He couldn't remember why he was there last time, but he was there. He asked his parents why he was there and they told him that he had been there because of an injury that he had from his guy named Karol. He could not remember Karol and asked them who that was. They were very worried because their son could not remember anything anymore. They called the main office of the hospital to hurry and check up on Ward House. The nurse came immediately to check up on Ward.

She tells his parents, "He will be in the hospital for at least another 3 days to do all the tests on him."

His dad had to call his boss because his son had to stay in the hospital another 3 days from a short term memory loss.

His boss realized that Ward was injured and tells the dad of Ward, "Ok you have vacation and you are there until your son is well rested, ok."

Ward's dad says, "Thank you, Sir."

He then went to get food to eat and asked Ward if he wanted something. He did want something. So he tells him that he wants a plate of eggs, hash brown, English muffin, pancakes, and a drink.

Chapter 8

That morning, Karol got out of his secret place and finally decides to find Ward and kill him even if it meant that he might get killed or get caught by the police. Karol first goes for the weapons so he goes to his uncle's house to find some in the basement. Good thing the basement door was opened and he got in and out like that. He first gets some more money from the safe and could only find a handgun with 6 bullets in it. Jack woke up from the couch and was hearing noises so he went down there very cautiously and quickly. He found the door and safe opened. Jack ran outside, but could not see anyone in sight. He thought it was Karol again that was stealing stuff again. Karol was running towards a gun store and had an ID of his uncle.

Then when he entered the gun store he found some cops right there and hid in a bush. He waited until the cops left, but they did not leave until 3 hours later when they get called for a car accident. He then enters the store of guns and goes for a shotgun and bullets.

Karol asks the manager, "Can I buy the gun if I am 18 years old? This was a lie."

The store guy tells him, "Well, we need the proof, but we also need the money for the store not to close down, so yes you can buy it."

Karol then rapidly got his stuff and brought the shotgun with equipment he needed. Karol then got the bag that he had brought and put everything in the bag. He then left to his secret place.

When he got there the cops were outside of his secret place and whispers to himself, "Man, I wish they had not found me because I do not have anywhere else to go. I can go to my first house. So he did that."

He had to do something so he decided to go there and left in a stolen car that he had got. The cops went inside Karol's place and found that someone was living there. They found clothes, raw food, the smell of pee and poop, the place with rats and snakes, and they also found some guns and knives. The cops were looking around for other stuff and found bullet shots on a wall. They looked and examined the clue.

Meanwhile the cops were right there, Karol was going to his old house and could not open the front door because it was hard to open. He used a knife to cut the door and it worked after about 1 hour. Karol got in and remembered the memories that he had in that house with his parents. He also found a picture book that had pictures of his parents. He almost cried to see them, but could not do that because he had to move or else the cops might find him. Karol started to look for a special weapon that was from his dad. His dad had told him that he would give him this weapon when the time was right. He did not know what he was looking for, but he saw the weapon in a box, a few years back. Karol was looking fast and made a mess, but finally he found a box on the very top of a counter. He saw that it needed a key to open it, but did not have the time so he used the shotgun to blow up the lock. He goes to the basement to test the weapon so that nobody would hear a sound. Karol starts by shooting some bullets then shot some more, but nothing happened. He started to get really mad and went crazy with the shotgun and shot it a lot of times on to the wall. Karol was now furious because it would still not open. He then thought of something which was to look for a key in a cabinet or in a secret place. Karol was looking so fast that he could not even see what he was going through in that basement.

He eventually, finds the key, which was a small scratched up key, but hoped it would still open the box. Karol was surprised when it opened and it was an explosive rocket launcher. He then thought what he can do with this thing in his possession. Then he knew what he had to do. He had to destroy Ward and go to jail if necessary. He then left with the special gift and with three missiles. Karol used a car which was stolen to get to the hospital.

Jack went to work in the morning and when he went to the restroom he heard a lot of noise. He got out and ran outside, he looked at one of the televisions and saw Karol on it. He was terrorizing the city with his rocket launcher. Jack knew that it was his brother's rocket launcher and Karol found it to destroy Ward. He contacted the hospital about a kid that was armed and heading there. So they told them to get Ward out of there.

In the hospital, Ward's dad had just received bad news about his brother. His brother had died 3 days ago and tells the nurse, "Why didn't they contact him earlier."

The nurse did not respond and tells him, "We did not know your cell phone number."

Ward's dad threw the phone from the angry he had and tells Ward about his uncle dying. Ward could not believe it because he could have told Karol about the misunderstanding. Ward could not tell Karol that Ward's uncle did the murder because there was no one to say it was true. Ward had to come up with something else because Karol would not believe who killed his parents anymore. His dad was crying, but was mad at the same time from what had happened. He could not believe it either.

Meanwhile in the city, Karol had destroyed houses and cars plus people with one shot. He was amazed by the beauty of this powerful machinery. Karol could not be stopped by anyone because he went in this store that sold rocket missiles and stolen them all. Karol knew that he could blow up the entire city with these missiles. The police start to approach the dangerous Karol with his heavy weapons.

They tell Karol, "Boy, you can just surrender or we will use force."

Karol just looked at them and smiled. He put a missile on his rocket launcher and blew up the police cars and people with one shot. The police had to call for reinforcement, but Karol launched another missile at them. It looked like Karol had cleaned up the street. Karol heads towards the hospital, but then when he got there his uncle Jack was there.

Karol aggressively says, "Jack get away from here before I blow up your brains with this thing, leave!"

Jack bravely says, "Karol I cannot let you kill a boy that did not do anything towards you family or you."

Karol impatiently says, "Jack I am not sorry, I will remember this day when I killed you on this day and Ward!"

Karol then used his rocket launcher and blew up Jack.

Jack before he got killed says, "Son, I know it has been a tough time, but just turn in yourself before you do something dumb."

Karol just laughed when he killed his uncle and says, "Finally, for the grand finale."

Karol entered the hospital and started to blow up rooms and rooms.

Karol then asked one of the nurses, "Which room is Ward House in?"

One nurse scared tells him, "In room 231."

He started to go there immediately. When he got there Ward was gone and Karol got mad. He then blew up more rooms and the hospital was crumbling down with 6 massive explosions. Karol then left and asked people if they had seen a boy named Ward. The people just ran away from him and Karol used another 3 more missiles on the hospital. He had to leave and find him, but when an old mad tells him that Ward was heading over to a safe zone with the CIA and the FBI. They were taking Ward's family and him to a safe zone until everything was clear to come out.

Karol was now really mad and had to do one thing which was to destroy everything as possible before he goes to jail. He knew that if he would even go where Ward was heading the cops and everyone would take him down. Karol before he left to die out there he remembered the last time he had family time. Karol then started to use the rocket launcher on the tallest building of New York and took down the other twin tower. Karol had destroyed about 9 towers and the cops were too afraid to stop him. Karol was so happy, but was mad that Ward had escape from his hands and could not get him again. He thought if he would turn himself in he would suffer, but if he commits suicide then he would not suffer. Karol, after a lot of destruction, just stood there when a tower he had taken down, and smashed his body onto the concrete.

Finally, after a lot of hours, the police were warned about the suicide of Karol Jason and the police tell Ward and his family that it was safe to come out. Ward was really sad to see a guy kill himself from someone that did not do anything with the killing of Karol's parents. The people of the city saw a lot of people killed and destruction everywhere they looked. Karol if he was alive would have been fined with 1st and 2nd degree murder, terrorism, and about another 150 charges on him. Ward could not believe Karol's uncle also got killed and he knew that Karol killed him too. Ward's parents were very fright, worried, scared to see a kid kill so many people and destroyed the city. After some days of counseling, Ward got back to going to school and his parents went to work again.

They then had a normal world again, but still with a lot of bad people. Ward was just happy that the case was closed of Karol Jason and Ward did not need to worry about another kid trying to kill him and his family.

Ward eventually got out of school and started to work on his dream job which was to work as a CIA agent. He then moved back to Cuba because there was a similar case over there. Ward lives with his own family and has a nice house. He now tells his coworkers and kids about the tragic day that was very scary. Ward is now investigating a lot more cases and likes to solve all of the cases there is in the world.

www.ingramcontent.com/pod-product-compliance
Lightning Source LLC
Chambersburg PA
CBHW021443170526
45164CB00001B/375